we are
no longer
the smart
kids in
class

FIRST POETS SERIES 14

Canada Council for the Arts

Conseil des Arts du Canada

ONTARIO ARTS COUNCIL
CONSEIL DES ARTS DE L'ONTARIO
an Ontario government agency
un organisme du gouvernement de l'Ontario

Canada

Guernica Editions Inc. acknowledges the support of the Canada Council
for the Arts and the Ontario Arts Council. The Ontario Arts Council
is an agency of the Government of Ontario.

We acknowledge the financial support of the Government of Canada.
Nous reconnaissons l'appui financier du gouvernement du Canada.

we are no longer the smart kids in class

David Huebert

GUERNICA
EDITIONS
TORONTO · BUFFALO · LANCASTER (U.K.)
2015

Michael Mirolla, general editor
Elana Wolff, editor
David Moratto, cover and interior design
Guernica Editions Inc.
1569 Heritage Way, Oakville, (ON), Canada L6M 2Z7
2250 Military Road, Tonawanda, N.Y. 14150-6000 U.S.A.
www.GuernicaEditions.com

Distributors:
University of Toronto Press Distribution,
5201 Dufferin Street, Toronto (ON), Canada M3H 5T8
Gazelle Book Services, White Cross Mills, High Town, Lancaster LA1 4XS U.K.

First edition.
Printed in Canada.

Legal Deposit—Third Quarter
Library of Congress Catalog Card Number: 2015940708
Library and Archives Canada Cataloguing in Publication

Huebert, David B., author
We are no longer the smart kids in class / David
Huebert. -- 1st edition.

(First poets series ; 14)
Issued in print and electronic formats.
ISBN 978-1-55071-957-4 (paperback).--ISBN 978-1-55071-958-1
(epub).--ISBN 978-1-55071-959-8 (mobi)

I. Title. II. Series: First poets series (Toronto, Ont.) ; 14

PS8615.U3W43 2015   C811'.6   C2015-903630-5   C2015-903631-3

CONTENTS

for my early readers:
Elizabeth, Rachel, Ron

to my manuscript in the slush pile

I hope you are comfortable, and that your neighbours
are mediocre at best. I hope your margins are crisp
as the day I hit print and cradled you while you emerged,
still warm, from your noisy womb. I'll never forget the

moment I wrapped the manila blanket over your shoulders
and lovingly snipped that excess length of packing tape.
I hope there has been no coffee spilled on you and that
you aren't too close to the radiator. These days I'm sure
there's no second-hand smoke, but I picture it nonetheless.

The editor is male—fifties, thick glasses, broom moustache.
He picks you up first thing in the morning, and as he reads
your name a smile crosses his lips—he already appreciates
your dry sense of humour and your understated brilliance.
He wets his index finger, turns the title page, and embarks.

why our parents worked so hard

You catch the spider
between a water glass
and a piece of paper.

You put it on the table.
It's a big one, about the size
of a head of garlic.

It feels its way around the space,
soon realizing there's no way out.

It stands still, clever thing,
to preserve the oxygen.

You light the joint
and lift the glass.

You blow a steady stream of smoke
and put the glass back down.

You watch the spider
forget how to walk.
It stumbles and slows.

A few minutes pass.
The spider stops moving.
You are asleep on the couch.

hearing rilke's *sonnets to orpheus*

Silence and ears, flowers and tongues.
The drone of muteness:
this odd sad song is steeped in it.

Let us listen to what the song
drowns out. Let us, like good
Heideggerians, tape our mouths
and cultivate the ring of stillness.

While we're at it, let us hear
these words as gerunds, not nouns —
beginning, opening, ending —
and preserve the process, catch it in a stutter.

Now pull off the tape, sing again —
sing the toneless, odd-volumed song
of the deaf. And rejoice. Revel in discord,
this grotesque limp of a tongue.

answering rilke's *sonnets to orpheus*

Sadness of all life, life of all sadness —
pouring death into fourteen lines,
you poured it well, smooth and steady,
twisting just so to catch the drip.

But I pity your ecstatic butterfly —
clutched in the grip of some poetic hiccough,
arrested flutter of the diaphragm.

I pity your fountain mouth,
your sleeping ear,
your blackened, aging chin.

And I pity your monuments,
so lonely, so unerected.

I pity the lyre — its indefinite,
soundless echo. Its player:

tired fingers, tired eyes,
nothing more to look back for,
yet the song goes on.

to a beer-swillin' poet

Hey man, I know it's dank and dreary,
down where you made your bed,
but I just thought I'd write to let you know,
not much has changed.

The drunk tank is still much the same.
Smells like piss and poetry.
No mattress, just a cold bench on an August night.
There's a bunch of us in here,
the others bang away on the plexiglass, whining,
"I'm not even drunk, I didn't even do anything!"

The one guy uses his best sober-business-man voice to say,
"I'm the assistant manager of a restaurant."
The cop is unimpressed.

Down the hall they bang and holler,
bang and holler.
If dogs in the pound could speak
it wouldn't make much difference,
this is how they'd sound.

There's a shirtless man stretched across the floor,
napping with cherubic half-moon mouth.
He's got matted curls for a pillow—better than concrete.
The other guys, they call him Jesus and 'Hey-Zeus.'
They laugh and laugh.

Turns out the one guy manages a Wendy's in Stellarton.
Another guy asks if I've got a cigarette.
I show him the nicotine patch on my arm,
offering it with a smirk.

One by one they let them out,
the great drunk tank exodus of 2009.
First Jesus, 'Hey-Zeus,' or Michael,
as the officer calls him.
They're old friends.
We're all friends in here.

First Michael is gone,
then the one guy,
then the other,
and I'm alone with the fluorescent lights.
They tell you to sleep it off,
beneath lights that stab your brain.
Maybe I'm not drunk enough.
Down the corridor the dogs bang and howl,
bang and howl.

I'm taking a leak when he comes, the officer.
A plexiglass rap denotes his watchful eye.
My guardian, my protector.
As he opens the door I feel the urge
to tell him: I'm not even drunk,
I didn't even do anything.

"Come with me please."
He escorts me down the hallway.
Hope mounts as we pass one cell,
then another, then the next.
They're all empty.
We stop.

On the left is the cell with the snarling dogs.
They're pressed against the door, banging and yelling,
banging and yelling,
four angry bodies in this little cage.
Now five.

I sit with a grunt and a growl.
We swap stories, explain that we're all innocent and sober.
The pack solidifies.
Me, sleeping guy (there's always one), French guy,
Native kid, and skinny guy.
We're buddies.

Soon French guy starts pounding his knuckles on the wall,
barking and snarling, scuffing his feet.
Native kid gets up to take a leak.
This is when the fun starts.
He lets out a long stream,
somewhere between the puke-encrusted toilet seat
and the bench.

French guy is livid.
He screams and curses, bares his teeth.
Bangs on the glass and yells,
"He's fuckin *pissin'* on the floor in here!"
With his bare feet, jumping in the piss-pool,
sloshing the puddle under the door,
trying to kick it at the cops —
watching, regulating.

This is when the fun starts.
Sleeping guy stands up, dazed.
Slowly gets his bearings. A big boy.
Swings at Native kid, then French guy;
they're both face-down in the piss, bleeding.
He bounds over to skinny guy,
starts pummelling his ribcage.
I cringe in the corner, feet on the bench,
flinching with the swings and splashes of piss and blood.

Sleeping guy turns, huge fists clenched — glares at me.
Eyes out of focus, frenzied.
There's no point to pleading,
all he sees is a heavy bag.

I try to remember your poem as I raise my palms,
but all I can think of is my teeth.
He turns back to skinny guy and starts on him again.
It's not pretty, but it's not me.

After a few minutes,
when everyone in the cell but me is nicely tenderized,
the cops come in.
Sleeping guy swings in all directions.
It only takes a taze or two to get him down.
Then the officer looks at me, the one who checked me in,
said it wouldn't be long because I wasn't very drunk.
His face bleeds recognition.
His face says, "I'm sorry," the only apology I'll receive.

He leaves, comes back—lets me out.
I don't mention it.
He knows, I know. There's really nothing to say.
As I leave, something compels me to blurt, "Thanks officer."

We're all friends in here.

roland

O, Roland, with your fat cheeks
that always glowed red, I'm sorry.

Sorry I stole your girlfriend
in high school, stole her like an unneeded
base, just for the joy of the steal.

That night she said both my names —
first and last, over and over.

Reminded me of the time they called
it out through the PA, when I scored
that game-winning goal.

Same leapfrog of pride and shame.
Same urge to be nameless, alone.

A few lurches and we were finished.
I put my pants on and she went back.
Back downstairs, to the party, and you.

christina

O, Christina, with your Kalamata skin
and your bold black eyes, I'm sorry.

Sorry we stole into some little-brother-bedroom
while Roland stayed downstairs smoking joints
and bragging, like he always did, about you.

I liked him but I'd never been with a girl
so dark and soft and beautifully swollen.
You were like a cello, just as sad and amber.

I made a joke. Your eyes flashed, and I knew.
I'm sure it sounds foul and misogynistic, but that's
how I was back then. I'm sorry for that too.

Mostly I'm sorry I couldn't see too well in the
liquor-drenched darkness, sorry I didn't play your
strings more sweetly, sorry we only had that

one time and when I ran into you a few weeks later
you said yes you were still with Roland, no you didn't
remember anything. And that maybe that was true.

the porn we watched

We talked about the porn we watched.
It felt good, it felt good
to know that someone else liked
something secret, sacred, foul.

I liked men with enormous
feet, you liked girls with hair
on their chins and it felt good,
it felt good to tell each other

this was okay, even kind of cool.
We were ten, neither one of us
capable of producing anything.
But we masturbated, oh we masturbated,

and it felt good, it felt good to thrash
and sweat side by side with a sweet
Catholic boy (your mother's mealtime
chant still rolling through my mind:

"Hands hands hands, thank you
God for hands"). We weren't sure
what would happen but we knew
it would be something huge, something

delightfully wrong. And of course
we were caught, shamed, and barred
from walking to school with the cool boys.
And even that, in its way, felt good.

ridiculous gods

When you were seven your father
told you you'd never make the NHL.

You cried then, you wailed to your gods —
Pavel Bure, Kirk Muller, Ron MacLean.

Your father gasped and clung to the wheel.
He cried to his gods too —
Ken Dryden, Peter Gzowski, John Donne.

The world unfolded as it does: you took your MA
in English, received funding and accolades,
prepared to join the family business.

You became a phenom of Friday night pickup,
chased the scoring race in the Thursday men's league.

And that classmate — the one who was drafted
but couldn't quite make the cut, whose talents

you coveted with a crazed, disorienting
lust, who wasn't quite Sydney Crosby
but played several years of Swedish pro —

you remember how at junior high practice
his dad always said, "At least they're having fun,"
and you forgive your father and his ridiculous gods.

in case you were wondering

The first step was losing the trench coat.
Then you came to Shakespeare class
bare-nailed and stripped of eyeliner.
A week later the lipstick was gone.

It wasn't that you were turning your back
on your postpunk roots.
You were simply becoming a poet.
Not like Ginsberg or Bukowski,
you were more the English Breakfast type.

You began to talk about Larkin,
measure your Scotch by the finger.
You started putting *after Ted Hughes*
beneath the titles of your poems.

You didn't know I was on the bus
the day I heard you speaking at full volume
about enjambment, metonymy,
and the gustatory image.

You used the word prosody
several times in a sentence,
and that was enough.

The sweater-vest was too much.
Soon it was a moustache, a bowtie,
and a wispy, grad student girlfriend.

By the end there was no need to tell me —
I knew. I wouldn't be receiving any more
of your late night texts.

But, in case you were wondering,
I haven't deleted them.
And from time to time I still
show this one around at parties:

I want to hunt your Moby Dick all night.
Love, Captain Ahab.

ideal first date

This date won't
end at eleven.
It will last a lifetime.
There will be waterfalls
of strawberries,
champagne crescendos,
days full of cuddling,
nights brimming
with unwanted mornings,
hearts beating together
like scrambling eggs
or dangling metronomes,
genitals always aroused
and never sated,
slow horseback rides
on private beaches,
tropical moonsets,
wild-eyed sunrises,
and sprawling oceans of lust.
There will be no exchange
of venereal disease.
Babies will come
exactly when they're
wanted, grow up
hale and taut —
obedient versions of us.

When we die
we'll learn
that there is a God,
we are the elect,
and there's no divorce
in eternity.

alabama

The first time I kissed her
it tasted like milk
and I remember
wanting not to forget
how she told me to close my eyes,
and drool less.

She was from Dartmouth.
We called her Alabama.

She was a veteran
of junior-high exploits,
familiar with dark basements,
absent parents,
and going almost all the way.

I recall a paternal baritone
buzzing through the walls,
a hastily tied ponytail,
jeans sliding over trembling hips,
a stubborn pubic hair,
a pillowcase drenched
in vanilla-laced sweat.

When it finally happened,
the power was out,
and I remember
her lightning-lit body
squatting on the bed,
her shrill laughter,
the half-hard snail
between my legs.

Then the lights flicked on,
exposing our sad pale bodies.

A shame, I thought
how everything looks uglier
under artificial light.

carnival

The Ferris wheel reaches its peak,
sputters, and stops.
There's no way down, so I dangle.

I observe with blunt pencils
and dry, ungenerous pens.
Mnemonic butter flies in my stomach:

all those times I said I couldn't sleep there,
said I had to work in the morning,
walked the night with sticky loins.

All those times I avoided public places,
quickly withdrew my hand.
I put my phone on silent,

trying to fool myself for a while.
When I open it there's no missed call,
no trace of her—just a laughing screen.

saturated doze

You dreamt about me
as I lay beside you,
our sated bodies braided.

You were rollerblading,
I was riding a skateboard
with eight wheels.

A professor's son,
a dentist's daughter —
we found a space
beyond the innocuous.

We pushed and clawed
past the picket fences,
chewed through the doors
of the two car garage.

Afterwards, I didn't dream.
I lay awake and worshipped —
your curls, your freckles,
your calm brown skin.

I couldn't face
the drone of sleep,
lest it numb me
from my unbelieving.

pubic decorum

She held firm convictions about pubic hair.
She believed, for example, that North American
women started shaving around the eighties,
when the shorn look was popularized in adult films.

She could tell you about fleas and crabs and merkins —
pubic wigs dating back to 1450, worn by working girls
to hide bald pelvises (shaven to ward off the lice).

She maintained that the French let their tufts grow
indefinitely and that in China, where fathers
accompany adult daughters to the baths,
it's shameful for unmarried girls to trim or shave.

She was not a proponent of the unkempt bush,
nor did she advocate a fully shaven loin.
She found bare genitals too puerile, too premature.

She preferred to keep a small, well-groomed patch,
like a carefully manicured front lawn —
causing thumbs and thighs to brush those coarse remnants,
the rough trappings of adulthood.

arriving at greenwood, greenwood station

The city collapses like a slovenly lover,
fully serviced. I roll away but it grunts
and follows, oozing unwanted warmth.

Below, the subway rumbles.
Traffic rolls through glutenous night.
Heat climbs in the window,
stirring this batter of bedroom air.

Two weeks and it's come to this:
bare walls and a caseless pillow.
I look out the window and laugh.
Never seen so many bicycles.

reading bowering's imaginary poems

Must be nice to be so lost.
After thirty-seven years she leaves you—
legs broken and no wheelchair.
Must feel good to grieve so deep.

My Angela lies beside me now,
naked back against
reading-lamp glare and body heat
on this who-would've-guessed

September night. I take her in,
guzzling wine glasses of hip,
gut lurching on half-pipe cusp.
One year. I want thirty-six more.

what i will remember most
about christmas 2011

is you drinking cough syrup in the nude.
That was the year you spent the holidays
with my family for the first time,
the year we picked up the tree
from the Superstore because my mother was sick
with mononucleosis. My father thought
I should have haggled more, thought forty bucks
was too much to spend on a tree.
He was probably right.
That was the year my sister had a new product
to make it look like there was no grease in her hair,
so she didn't have to shower as much.
This was always her way. Back when she was a smoker
she liked to say she preferred menthols
so she didn't have to brush her teeth.
That was the year you called these bizarre people
your new family. You and I spent days
coughing and curling up on couches
in the basement, huddling beneath blankets,
the terriers sleeping on our laps,
kicking their way through doggy dreams.
That was the year we knocked
the mucus off each other's lungs
with karate chopped shoulder blade rhythms
and lathered our chests with Vaporub,
the year you read *The Picture of Dorian Gray*
and we made it halfway through the film *Dorian Gray*.
That was the year my mother bought iPads

for my sister and me, just so she could see our faces
on the other side of the country.
My dad and I stayed up reading Wallace Stevens,
trying to figure out what he meant
by the emperor of ice-cream.
That was the year, once we got better,
I played "Brown Eyed Girl" and you said,
You hate that song, and I said, with a grin: *I know.*
That was the year we walked the snow-coated trails
of Point Pleasant Park in the waning sunlight,
gazed at the popsicle-pink sky
crowning the corpses of spruce trees —
the ones that were crippled by the longhorn beetle
and finished by Hurricane Juan.
You said you'd never seen the park so beautiful,
pristine and regal in its white winter cloak.
The trails unfolded before us like winding carpets
and every footstep birthed a different sound.
That was the year we lost the dog.
Darkness fell heavy and fast and we were still calling,
helplessly, *Here Py! Here Py!*
our voices drenched in desperation.
Your eyes close to tears. Shivering.
The cold severity of the Atlantic
hanging thick as slabs of bacon fat.
We traded tight-jawed glances, sharing, as always,
the burden of each other's fear.
That year there had been coyote sightings in the park.
You said, *We can't go home without your sister's dog.*
Later I realized this was the first time you'd called it home.
Go home? I said. *If we don't find her we'll be here all night.*
Of course I'll never forget

the sight of Py trotting back slowly,
apprehensively, her little white body
barely visible on the snowy path,
pausing now and then to cringe
and turn her head away in shame.
I'll never forget the euphoria in my fingers
as I clipped the leash onto her collar.
We turned, the three of us, back to the car. Together.
But what I will remember most is you,
naked in the full light of the bedroom,
raising the spoon to your mouth.
Your whole body squirming
against the taste.

a couple of bikes

The bikes wintered in the living room.
Not in the lofty, Seinfeldian sense —
mounted on the wall, backdropping
zany kitchen scenes. These bikes
were cast aside, forgotten behind an
armchair no one sat in. They passed

the season soaking in the coldness
of the room, a poorly insulated
afterthought that overhung the porch.
They faced all the draughts
of Greenwood Avenue. Mud dried
on their tires as grease thickened in

the chains. All winter I passed them,
dragging my hockey gear bashfully
across the floor. Had they been dogs
the bikes would have huffed and raised
their pleading eyes, knowing full well
they would not be coming on this drive.

cadaver on bloor street

Observe the skeleton.
Still fastened to the post, intact u-lock
mocking purpose itself, like a torn
body bag luffing against a corpse.

Machine denied proper burial,
left to rot in shame, like Polynices
on the battlefield of Thebes.
O, Bicycle, where is your Antigone?

Desecrated, dewheeled, stripped
of handlebars, pedals, seat, and chain.
The dogs and the carrion
have sent you naked to the afterlife.

This rusting frame, these exposed sinews.
Seatpost cast upwards against the sky —
an indicting finger levelled
on the shrugging, high-noon sun.

black ice, crowsnest pass

I'd never seen hills like these—transport tucks chugging
up preposterous gradients, looking hopeless and laughable,
their tired engines whirring as they scaled the fault line of
the planet itself.

It was January, the sky thick with rank wetness: cavalcades
of rain and snow, snow and rain, water mutating into
windshield ooze as we gasped up mountain after moun-
tain and clenched—lungs, bowels, bladders.

The wiper blades were long past useless, squeaking and
flapping against the glass as I struggled to keep the Buick
at seventy. Passing trucks. Torrents of grey-brown high-
way splash.

Around midnight we dipped into the big, yawning salad
bowl of Osoyoos Valley. Relief. No moisture in sight.
Hammering toe into gas, I pounced on the strip of clear,
dry pavement. The Buick launched up and out, shooting
through inclines, careening around x-rated curves, steadily
rising into the cloudless sky.

We felt good, alone with the vacant night, our eyes
jumping in time with the yellow drumbeats in the middle
of the road. Darkness had never looked so sexy. We turned
the music up as we reached the peak, the Buick soaring at
an effortless one-thirty.

Then we hit the descent. The entire mountain dropped off beneath us as we launched around a corner and hit a sheer, sprawling straightaway—the road levelled at the centre of the earth. The yellow drumbeats passed faster and faster as we charged into the cavernous below. I stepped on the brakes, and—nothing.

I tried again. No response. The front of the Buick drifted towards the mountain wall, back wheels swung around behind. I took my foot off the brake and waited. Tried again.

A lifetime of jubilation as the tires gripped the road. I slowed the Buick to sixty, reached over to the passenger seat, clutched her wrist to be sure it was there.

We almost died just now, I said.
She chuckled and played with my hair.
I'm not ready to say goodbye to you yet, she joked.

We found a motel in Grand Forks, took primal slumber between mice-scritching walls. In the morning we bought a new set of wipers.

elegy for a buick century

January on the Crowsnest,
half an hour east of Salmo.
The sun was bright, the road crisp
as we headed up Kootenay Pass.

The Buick had a few problems:
warped rotors, bent axles,
worn callipers, chunky transmission,
and a whining catalytic convertor.
But we figured she'd make the drive.

Natasha stroked my cheek
and I held her thigh as we sang
Motown songs and climbed.

Around noon the sun darted off,
leaving a thick grey ceiling above the white carpet
of the road. I had to brake around every corner,
suck deep breaths to keep my stomach down.

A tight switchback and we found
a line of brake lights glowing through the gloom.
Later we'd learn an avalanche
had smeared the road, traffic was stalled
while the highway crew cleared the debris.

I stepped on the brakes and as the tire-rumble
quieted I thought I heard something,
turned the music down and there it was,
a hectic popcorn rattle beneath the hood.
Soon smoke was pumping out of the engine,
thick, black, and violent.

I jumped out, lifted the hood,
saw the bubbling coolant—
fluorescent green,
churning at a steady boil.

Before I could start feeling sorry for myself
two men approached,
all smiles and plaid and thick leather gloves.
One was sixty with salt-and-pepper handlebars,
the other was thirty-something
with mutton chops and pale blue eyes.

They leaned into the engine.
"Where ya comin' from?"
"Where ya to?"
"How's the rad?"
"Temp gauge working?"

They fired off questions, prodding
the engine's intimates.
I watched, hunched against the cold,
answered what I could.

"They seem nice," Natasha said, burrowing into me.
We huddled together as the snow melted into our shoes,
watched Handlebar wrap his sweater
over his hand and feel around the radiator.
There was a hiss, a smell of burning plastic.
"Yep," he said, peering in and squeezing.
"She's hurtin'. Got any water?"

Between the coolant in my trunk
and the water in their Ford
they managed to stabilize the radiator.

We changed socks, put the seats back,
and leaned into one another,
passing the time with cold coffee
and peanut butter sandwiches.

Two hours later the line of pink smudges
lit up again. I was stunned when the Buick
turned over without a fuss.

Handlebar and Mutton Chops
looked under the hood.
"Buy yourself a lottery ticket," Handlebar said.
Mutton Chops grinned. "Drive 'er like you stole 'er."

We stayed close behind the Ford as we crept down the
        mountain.
Soon the slope levelled out, the sun broke through,
and a scalp of concrete gleamed through the ruts in the snow.
Handlebar waved as he stepped on the gas
and the Ford peeled away,
leaving us behind in the sun-soaked valley.

And the car? she made the drive —
past Creston, down to Fernie,
all the way to Calgary, and back.
In the end I sold her for three hundred bucks.
I heard the final stroke was a blown gasket
on a logging road near Smithers.
I figure if Handlebar and Mutton Chops had been there,
she would've made that drive too.

revenge of polyphemus

They say the coyotes walked
all the way to Newfoundland.
They followed the moose
across the ice
and if that's not love
love probably doesn't exist.

*

This year we stuck our thumbs
into the eye of winter.

We rode our bicycles
around the rotary,
blindfolded. You said
there's no such thing
as too much snow.

We took a bath,
washed each other's genitals.
It felt good but you went
a little heavy on the soap.

When you cut yourself
trimming your pubic hair
you had to shave one side,
I said your private parts
had never looked so trendy.

We were in Montreal
when a storm blew the roof
off our house.

On the drive back to Toronto
you told me to stop going on
about my life's work,

so I discussed the only other thing
I knew how to talk about:
the unmoved mover
of the uppermost moveable sphere.

Fucking Greeks, you said.
Who? I asked.
Nobody.
Nobody, you mean like Polyphemus?

You laughed and said,
If winter is a cyclops,
why do I have two thumbs?

That's when the moose
walked into the road,
glaring at us with his one huge eye.

I stepped on the brakes
but it was useless with these
goddamn hairy coyote feet.

As we skidded towards
that beautiful one-eyed moose
I imagined our roofless apartment
filling with sleet,
stacks of paper fluttering
through the kitchen.

I saw Poseidon there,
with the nymph Thoösa,
singing and making love
as the snow melted beneath them.
The moose looked at me and winked.

ruins walk, louisbourg

We share an apple on the point.
I carve Swiss Army slices while
angry waves gnaw the shore.

Wedges pinched between thumb
and blade. She munches idly,
toeing spiders in the sand.

The breeze holds all the rage of the
Atlantic. Traces of gunpowder
flare my history-tickled nostrils.

Beside us children in period dress
chase geese. Above is a sky
that has forgotten how to laugh.

equine tide, sailors memorial walk

A thousand angry horses
foaming at the mouth.

Behind them, a haven:
the stretching disc

where grey Atlantic sea
meets grey Atlantic sky.

Elysium.

The beasts reject this refuge,
choosing, instead, to face

the obstinate rocks.
One by one, spines twist, snap

and recoil — water, as always,
turning back on itself.

breaking

The season withers.
Snowpack goes temperamental,
soft and volatile in the afternoon sun,
crust of melt-freeze crackle in the pre-dawn gasp.

You are too small.
Time slides like a wet-snow avalanche.
A single finger takes hours to climb. Slopes burn
like infected genitals—pleasures pass but leave their mark.

It's time to go home.
Stern peaks offer no abode for summer.
The ocean whispers on your pillow, calling
you to join the dialogue: salty tongues, lips of shore.

You jog up a logging road, shouldered
by conifers. How they brood. The Lizard Range
licks around you, a horseshoe without an exit. Above,
the sun burrows through. Hard to break a sweat in this cold.

spring melt, fernie

Not nature,
because you're wary of the idea.

(Don't abide the poets
and their oil-slick whispers).

Not nature,
but a place to encounter elk,

marmots, eagles, and the
needle-sharp bite of glacial air.

A place where you find severity
on the sides of highways —

massive boulders of rotting snow,
filled with snapped branches,

uprooted trees, reminding you
that these vast surfaces

break off in slabs
and slide.

sailor's dictionary

The word hung decktop, woeful
as a young testicle in an ancient sack.
A cuatro, he called it, naming the space
between ukulele and mandolin.

O, the impotence of names. The captain
thumbed and plucked, waxing Hawaiian
while waves licked and spat up the hull.
We felt continental shifts in the space

between guacamole and refried beans,
took turns reading from the sailor's
dictionary. Somewhere between chicken
fruit (eggs) and grog blossoms (rum cheeks)

we turned around. The talk veered to salmon
and iron spinnakers (motors), and we wound up
back on land. Land, where there's less hope
for floating than in the betweens of sea.

impotence

You tell yourself there are words in your veins.
They mean so much more than the ones that make it onto
    the page.

You told yourself, so many times,
that words could make it stay.

You could write it all—her crooked left cheekbone, the
one eye slightly larger than the other, your father's
pillowy-sharp moustache, how you used to think the
texture of his stubble was what rhino skin would feel like,
the reason you didn't love her, the arguments you could
win only by clawing at old scabs, the way he half-limped
across the field, holding a bottle of malt liquor and a long
leash, the Rottweiler trotting in front of him, his frayed
black baseball cap lying crooked on his head, the piles of
blond cotton balls jumping out in every direction, his
expression, the look of a man who needed to be
written—you thought you could save it all.

Tomorrow you might learn
that this won't make it not go away.

fingernail clippings

An insect becomes a wish, and ladybugs away.
My reading lamp sheds light on an inchworm.
In the alms of dawn it glows and squirms,
in the evening it careens in centimetric sway

as fragile strawberries furnish dreams
with mould-soaked arteries; stigmas of decay.
A lawnmower spins and chokes (on a stump of finger).
When we eat egg whites, what happens to the yolks?

I carry a briefcase full of peanut butter
and put all my important documents in there.
I used to think what I wanted to think,
then I cut my hair.

radicals

We stand against
conformity.
We buy used clothes
in today's fashions.
We drive bicycles,
talk Chomsky, think
outside the sphere.
We do not go
to the gym or
the tanning bed.
We buy GREEN
toilet paper,
LOCAL produce,
ORGANIC
computers.
We brew our own
beer, compost
prodigiously.
Yes: our facial
hair *is* ironic.
We think critically
about everything.
We think highly
of ourselves. We
have created new
monsters — tight pants
and moustaches
for men, high-waisted
jeans for women,

plaid for both genders.
We do not see
people in terms
of gender.
We are artists —
mostly ugly
photographers
and photogenic
poets. We will not
abide the status quo.
We stand against
conformity.
Join us.

murderer's elegy

I am a man,
an ape, a clown.

I built my house on a mountain
and it's falling down.

*

I walk on streets
paved with bones.

I learned to fly
on the wings of cadavers.

I erected cathedrals,
straining light with blood-stained glass.

But bones will crumble
when Time sits on them.

Wings will fall
when they face the laughing wind.

Glass will shatter
when the screams reach the right decibel.

*

My gods have died
but I still pray,

I made my bed out of ashes
and it's blowing away.

hypothesis

When I am old
I will yearn
for non-electric
skateboards,

pine after
hovercrafts
that don't carry
conversations.

I will well up
remembering
the smell
of burnt petroleum,

dream of
the sounds
of airplanes

dropping bombs
before crashing
into mountains

which became
the smouldering
wreckage

out of which
I construct
this home.

social circle

There are no children in my social circle
anymore—
        (yet).

In a church sound travels up and up
and you can't convince me that it all
comes back down.

There are friends here, friends
I was never fond of,

and poets, there are poets too.
(I am fond of them but I can't
understand their work).

There is evidence for the flood:
fish fossils discovered
at the top of a mountain,

the Pioneer 10, complete
with 6 x 9 inch diagram
of the essence of humanity,

and me. I'm just reaching into
the great refrigerator of existence,
checking for leftovers.

the growth

Worst case scenario, it's a tumour.
She actually says that.

What have you been doing lately, for sex?
This is what the doctor says.

Now in addition to cancer
I'm thinking about herpes,
warts, the clap.

Next he tells me to drop my pants.
Examining my genitals he says,
Have you tried squeezing it?

I try squeezing it.
Pus lurches, like toothpaste from a fresh tube.

A pained smile.
It's a pimple, he says.

Back home she is happy, I am happy.
We have sex.
It's not the worst case scenario.

But she's way too proud afterwards,
when, all cute-post-coital-glow,
she grins and calls me "pimpledick."

the smart kids

The Yates Street Shell is the centre
of my universe. It breathes Lego red
and mustard yellow into the windows
of my capital-gee green neighbourhood.

At night the stars and the moon hide
behind this Nickelodeon miasma
as I bathe in the hemp-soap serenity
of British Columbian evenings.

Late night walks with like-minded
companions (a bearded Marxist
and a well-travelled farm girl) unearth
the agony of our graduate seminars:

We are no longer the smart kids in class.

Down the street there's a cedar that was
once the centre of this universe. Now its
leaves breathe gas station gleam while
unhomed deer gnaw its weary husk.

I don't notice, and if I did I wouldn't care.
When I round the corner past this tree and
glimpse the red beacon that never strays too far
from a dollar twenty-six, I know I'm home.

So I abide the fungus of unease as I slide
beneath the sheets and watch the lazy mating
dance of phosphorescence and glass,
forgetting to wonder who, if anyone, is at fault.

life after twitter

When Twitter suggested I follow @jacklayton
several months after he'd passed away
I got to wondering.

When I die, what will become
of these manifold manifestations of me,
this ethereal plurality, my online self?

Will people notice the conspicuous absence of tweets
or will my list of followers keep expanding,
becoming increasingly populated with names like
@juicybod367 and @phoebe_phuxalot?

What will happen to my emails?
Will my Hotmail inbox grow ever fatter,
swelling with offers of penis enlargements,
workout plans, dietary regimens,
and reminders to send birthday cards
to people I never cared for?

Will this make me wish,
even from the grave,
that I had been quicker
to make the change to Gmail?

Will my Facebook wall,
like some malignant tower of babble,
climb indefinitely towards the heavens?
Or will it reach a breaking point
somewhere near the mesosphere
when roboticized simulations
of Mark Zuckerberg's cerebral processes
finally figure out I'm dead?

I wonder if my last words will be a tweet
or perhaps a status update,
something horrifically quotidian, like:
"Is Prince a man or a woman?"

without a door

Quiet sex is fun till the finish.
That's when they start to hear it—
the clutched headboard rattle
the soft squelch of fluids
the sweat-muted clap
of thigh on buttock,
gut against gut.

Afternoons we lie gasping
while bodies, boots, long johns,
and dishes fill the living room, thick
as Guinness on a black and tan.

Evenings roll like weighted dice,
stumble like flakes
of zero degree snow.

After dinner we all play gin rummy,
talk about cliffs and flips.
Then two break off, shearing
like weak layers in a snowpack.

We go upstairs
to our doorless room
and fuck as quietly as we can.

Nothing changes
as we cover our mouths
and come.

twenty-four abandoned attempts at the beginning of my first novel

1) And then
2) Years later
3) The following day
4) Happily ever after
5) That was the night he put a gun in his mouth and
6) Susan looked up, mid-blowjob, and realized where she was — in the back of a taxi on the outskirts of Mexico City, giving head to an orangutan while a fourteen year-old girl in knee-high pumps took pictures from the passenger's seat. This was not good. The orangutan began to pleasure himself. The last thing Susan remembered was Calgary. The owner's box of the Saddledome. Someone inviting her to the dressing room to meet a couple of players. Jolli and Tikka? Their names meant nothing to her, but she'd heard they had a pretty good coke connection and were hung like giraffes with more girth. There was champagne and that rich perv with the plugs was leering at her tits. A girlfriend handed her a pill and then … This. She glanced at her reflection in the rearview. Her eyes looked like they'd been clawed at by bloodthirsty racoons for the past forty-eight hours. Her gaze flicked from the mirror to the road. Up ahead, some asshole was trying to veer through all six lanes to get to the other side of the freeway. A cacophony of horns fired up, sounding like a thousand gigantic anuses. Six or seven vehicles had to slam on the brakes and swerve to miss this lunatic. Then he

crashed into a motorcyclist, sending the poor bastard
careening into a spiral of unfathomable carnage. I
yanked on the emergency brake, slid into a U-turn.
The orangutan was coming

7] In the beginning was the

8] A long time ago in a galaxy

9] We were somewhere around Lethbridge on the edge
of the prairies when the beef began to take hold

10] It happened on the day I was facefucked by Jesus Christ

11] On the outskirts of Gotham City

12] In the depths of the Bat Cave

13] Alfred

14] Last night I fell asleep on the toilet again

15] I was always secretly in love with

16] My favourite kind of pornography involved

17] As a child I had a crush on this girl named

18] Leslie

19] Leslie was

20] My father

21] Cats

22] As I write this I'm surrounded by cats. Literally. There
are mountains of the fuckers, all around me. They're
all over my body — legs, neck, shoulders, head, hands.
I'm submerged in the undergrowth of a veritable feline
jungle. I can barely bring my hands to the keyboard.
This is what life is like in the year 3094. The smells are
unbearable — cat shit, cat piss, cat puke, cat semen, cat
food. Yes, they have cat food here. Don't ask me how,
but there are huge stockpiles of these little tins of wet
cat food, landfills overflowing with the dry stuff. To
tell you the truth, I haven't eaten anything but cat food
for the past eight years. I have no clue if they make

the stuff or, if not, where it comes from. One thing is clear: these things are smart. They're smarter than me, that's for sure. The great human brain is finally obsolete, vanquished, overthrown. Who would've thought? Cats. All you have to do is look into their godforsaken eyes to know how murderous they are. The expression is always the same — cold, cunning, implacable. They can sense how much I hate them, and they love it. Smug little bastards. Those eyes could drive a fella to the brink. I'd love to stick my thumbs right in there, pull those eyeballs out, eat them for dinner. Now that's desperation. I'd use their little food-tins for a plate. Right now about five hundred cats are rubbing their backs against me. The rest are clawing at my body. I'm a goddamn human scratching post here. I have to cover myself with layers of wool to prevent them from getting at my flesh. Needless to say, this gets pretty hot in summer. And it never ends. They never tire of their scratching, never relent from their torturous screams — Meow! Meow! Jesus. The ceaseless, harrowing clamour. It's unbearable. Sometimes I wish I could just end it all

23) Tonight I'm going to end it all

24) The end

shavings

Somewhere

there are words
on tongues,

tongues hanging
on trees
that can't be climbed.

Lead snaps and lodges
where shavings are cut
and discarded.

      Somewhere

a stump
still runs
along
a page.

notes

"To a Beer-Swillin' Poet": This poem responds to Al Purdy's "The Drunk Tank."

"Ridiculous Gods": For Ron Huebert.

"Saturated Doze": For Natasha.

"Reading Bowering's Imaginary Poems": This poem responds to George Bowering's "Imaginary Poems for AMB," which I encountered in the collection *Vermeer's Light* (Talonbooks 2010).

"What I will remember most about Christmas 2011": For Rachel and Py.

"Elegy for a Buick Century": For Brad Roach.

"Revenge of Polyphemus": For Elizabeth Edwards, who taught me and many others the Greeks.

"Equine Tide: Sailors Memorial Walk": The title refers to a walking path in Point Pleasant Park, Halifax.

acknowledgements

Previous incarnations of these poems appeared in the following publications:

The Antigonish Review: "Why Our Parents Worked So Hard," "Ridiculous Gods"; *Event*: "To a Beer-Swillin' Poet"; *Jones Av.*: "Shavings," "Impotence"; *Literary Review of Canada*: "Equine Tide, Sailors Memorial Walk," "Answering Rilke's *Sonnets to Orpheus*," "Ruins Walk, Louisbourg"; *Matrix*: "Twenty-Four Abandoned Attempts at the Beginning of my First Novel"; *Open Heart 6: Anthology of Canadian Poetry*: "Carnival"; *Open Heart Forgery*: "Murderer's Elegy"; *Ottawa Arts Review*: "Alabama"; *Poetry Is Dead*: "The Porn We Watched"; *Pulp Poems: poems on recycling, paper, and the environment*: "The Smart Kids," "Radicals," "Fingernail Clippings"; *Qwerty*: "Reading Bowering's Imaginary Poems"; *Vallum*: "Cadaver on Bloor Street."

This book owes great debts to the following places and individuals: my editor Elana Wolff and the terrific people at Guernica Editions, Natasha Bastien, Elizabeth Edwards, Ronald Huebert, Rachel Huebert, Py and Pandora, les Bastien, Aaron Kreuter, the boys from Halifax, the Bake Sale Collective, the Buick, the Kootenays, Gus' Pub, Centennial Arena, Point Pleasant Park.

about the author

A child of Halifax, Nova Scotia, David Huebert now lives in London, Ontario, where he is working on a PhD.

MIX
Paper from
responsible sources
FSC® C100212

Printed in August 2015
by Gauvin Press,
Gatineau, Québec